THE QUILT:

New Directions for an American Tradition
QUILT NATIONAL

Schiffer Publishing Ltd

Box E, Exton, Pennsylvania 19341

ACKNOWLEDGEMENTS

Pamela Parker, Executive Director, The Dairy Barn
David Norton, President, The Dairy Barn Board of Directors
Hilary Fletcher, *Quilt National '83* Coordinator
Doreen Strasser-Pallini, *Quilt National '83* Exhibition Designer
Suzy Chesser, Secretary
The Steering Committee:
    Virginia Beals, Sue Crook, Elaine Dawson,
    Mary Kaye Jordan, Judy Mayer, Mary Norton,
    Phyllis Rovner, Elaine Stecker, Natsu Taylor
The American Craft Museum, New York City
Fairfield Processing Corporation, makers of Poly-fil® Brand Batting; Danbury, Connecticut
The Ohio Foundation on the Arts
The Ohio Arts Council
The many Athens, Ohio, businesses and organizations that supported
Quilt National '83 and the many volunteers who contributed their
time, energy, and expertise.
The Ohio University School of Home Economics

COVER: Quilt #21, by Pam Studstill, San Antonio, Texas
        Best of Show: *Quilt National '83*

Cover and Book Designer: PORTER SMITH-THAYER
Editor: NANCY ROE
Photographer of Exhibition Quilts: C.H. MERKLE

Printed in the United States of America.
ISBN: 0-916838-92-7
Published by Schiffer Publishing Limited, Box E, Exton, Pennsylvania 19341

THE QUILT:

New Directions for an American Tradition

Quilt National '83 exhibition, installation. Photograph by Brian Blauser.

Terrie Hancock Mangat
Cincinnati, Ohio
Fishing Hats Over Rose Lake
Cotton blends, rose appliques, sequins. The hats have various plastic and rubber artifacts sewn on them; reverse appliqued. Photographed by Brian Blauser.

Award Winner:
MOST INNOVATIVE USE OF THE MEDIUM.

INTRODUCTION
About Quilt National

The past few years have seen such an increase in the number of artists engaged in contemporary quiltmaking; so many shows, books, and articles; such acceptance of the art form; such a growth industry in suppliers of materials, that it is difficult to recall that *Quilt National '79* happened only four years ago or that it had such impact.

It was created, just as were the works it displayed, from many individual pieces—a serendipitous coming together of the right people in the right place. In 1978, Nancy Crow, then living in Athens, Ohio, turned her creative energies and talent from weaving to contemporary quiltmaking. That same year, a group of Athens area residents succeeded in getting a magnificent slate-roofed 64-year-old barn included in the National Register of Historic Places and organized as an arts center, The Dairy Barn.

By 1979, Nancy Crow and other artists were seeking an outlet, a place to display the contemporary quilt to the public. When Dairy Barn representatives came to ask her to lead a workshop on quiltmaking, Crow countered with, "Why not an exhibition of contemporary quilts instead?"

And so *Quilt National '79,* the first juried national show of contemporary quilts, came into being.

The setting for the first exhibit, with quilts hanging near stanchions that once separated championship Holstein cows, gave the show even more impact. Another contrast that sharpened interest was that the exhibit came out of a region with a strong, unbroken history of traditional quiltmaking in such long-favored patterns as Grandmother's Flower Garden, Dresden Plate, Double Wedding Ring, and Nine-Patch.

Quilt National broke on the bucolic Southeast Ohio scene with 56 contemporary works by 44 quilt artists, selected from 390 works submitted by 196 artists. In some of the selections, viewers saw the geometrics and borders rooted in old, loved patterns; and many quilts displayed traditional patchwork and applique techniques.

Other entries startled viewers, who found themselves facing flesh-colored floating satin nudes, or color-Xeroxed chewing gum wrappers, or quilts made of handmade paper or brown paper bags.

Some quilts were like paintings transferred to cloth, with family ties to op, pop, minimal, and even funk art movements. Some had forgotten about neat edges and zigzagged off into space. At least two could be separated into units and assembled in different ways.

Some hit the eyes like full sunlight after darkness; others were equally surprising in their subtle use of color.

It would be stretching things a bit to compare the 1979 *Quilt National* with the famous 1913 Armory Show that turned the art world upside down, but it is true that some are still reeling from the shock of seeing grandmother's treasured craft turned into something so boldly new and various.

Interestingly enough, other viewers of the 1979 show were vocal in denouncing what they saw as artists clinging to the past, to the "cute" or safe image, and not going far enough, fast enough, to move quilt from bed to wall, from craft to art.

By *Quilt National '81,* the number of quilts submitted for jurying had risen 40 percent, and it was apparent that the contemporary quilt was coming into its own. This time, 78 quilts by 60 artists from 21 states and Canada were displayed. One obvious difference from the 1979 exhibit was the increasing number of techniques employed: silkscreen, block printing, stamping, Xerox-transfer, painting, cyanotype, lithography, and batik were all in evidence.

The Best of Show Award went to Pamela Jean Burg of Holley, New York, for "Curtain," a 30" by 30" framed work of color-Xeroxed paper and plastic that raised in many minds the question of when is a quilt a quilt.

Quilt National '83 gave space to 84 quilts by 79 artists from 40 states, Canada, and England. It is these works—selected from more than 700 entries—that form *The Quilt: New Directions for an American Tradition.*

What was apparent to those who had followed the evolution of the art was that in this third *Quilt National* the contemporary quilt had reached new levels of sophistication in design, exploration of color, and mastery of technique.

For the jurors—well-known quilt artists Francoise Barnes and Virginia Jacobs and Paul J. Smith, director of the American Craft Museum, *Quilt National '83* was an opportunity to take stock, to look at the state of the art, and to ask what would come next and who would lead the way.

Through its 84 color plates and its comments by the *Quilt National* jurors and by two leaders in this art form—Nancy Crow and Michael James—*The Quilt: New Directions for an American Tradition* records for this and future generations the state of this art at a particular place and time.

THE STATE OF THE ART

Artist Michael James at work. Photograph courtesy of the artist.

Michael James

The term "contemporary quilting" still conjures visions of young, tradition-defying reactionaries flying in the face of hundreds of years of well-worn and well-loved American needle art heritage. Purists still man the barricades at the mere mention of machine quilting, and the introduction of foreign matter such as paper or plastic is the stuff of revolution.

The popularity of quiltmaking has grown by leaps and bounds in the last 15 years, and its viability as an art medium has been enhanced, but the realist knows that the expressive potential of this medium has barely begun to be realized.

When I first became interested in quilts and in making them, I decried the fact that as late as the third quarter of the 20th century quilts were still viewed as "women's pastime," as "needlecraft," as second-rate art. Others joined in berating the chauvinisms that had kept quiltmaking isolated from other modern art forms. With surprising speed we seem to have turned heads and changed attitudes, and, in the bargain, I think we've created a monster.

Now, in the 1980s, *all* quilts seem to be art, and *all* quilters are artists. Quilters everywhere are seriously "expressing" themselves with needle and thread, merrily rolling along toward the 21st century as they see themselves creating a new legacy for future generations.

I'm inclined to jump off the bandwagon at this point and take a more critical view of the situation. What I encounter as I look around at quiltmaking in 1983 is much less innovation than imitation. Old quilt patterns, though now more frequently disguised in one way or another, still form the basis for 90 percent of the work being produced by quiltmakers today. The orientation to this art form remains, for the most part, 19th century in nature. The license to copy patterns that helped to define what quiltmaking was 100 years ago seems still,

unfortunately, to define it today. I suspect that is one reason why, even among the other 10 percent, we see so many imitations and "take-offs" that refer to work by a relative handful of quilt artists who are doing the actual trailblazing.

If the work of these few artists is influencing a new generation of quiltmakers, what, then, influences this handful of trailblazers?

Historical quilts, to be sure, play a large part in the contemporary quilt artists' approach to their work, but they are seen not as standards against which to measure up but as documents detailing the intellectual and emotional responses of artists at another time to different sets of social, political, and cultural stimuli. The quilt artist would no more copy or imitate these than the serious modern painter would the works of Titian, Rembrandt, or Picasso.

Other visual art forms such as painting, weaving, film, and photography (in both their historical and contemporary manifestations) are constantly providing stimulation to artists working with the quilt, and their work stimulates artists in those other media. I think it would be fair to say that serious contemporary quilt artists are as aware of developments in other media as they are of trends in their own disciplines.

Perhaps the single most deciding influence that shapes the work of contemporary quilt artists, however, is that impulse to be a maverick, to be an individual and to produce individual work, that is shared either consciously or subconsciously by all "trailblazers." They are not satisfied with the past—with the known—but look to the unknown, searching in uncharted lands, mapping their own courses, and writing their own guidebooks.

Exhibits such as *Quilt National* offer some of them the chance to present their private explorations and discoveries, the fruits of labor carried on

Artist Nancy Crow in her studio outside Baltimore, Ohio. Photograph courtesy of Amy Sencetta. Reproduced with permission of The Columbus Dispatch, Columbus, Ohio.

in isolated studios, to the world of quilt enthusiasts.

—Michael James

Michael James has participated in all three *Quilt National* exhibitions, serving as juror for the first and workshop leader for the second and third. Acknowledged as one of contemporary quilt-making's leading figures, James is the author of *The Quiltmaker's Handbook* and *The Second Quiltmaker's Handbook*.

Nancy Crow

What I think is happening in the contemporary quilt world is that, since no college or university offers a degree in this art, most quiltmakers learn from others through what must be one of the most organized networks of artists ever to exist. This may account in part for the derivative elements that Michael James mentions.

It's also true that some of the most effective and creative quilt artists are also the most effective and creative teachers. This means not only that they will have an influence but also that teaching, writing, and administrative detail take time from the artist's work. Work *is* in progress, but there are zones of time when there will not be a lot of new work coming out.

The quiltmaking process is so slow that it takes an artist a long period to establish a body of work, and there will inevitably be the dry periods common in all the arts. We can't expect constant new and exciting work, any more than we can in other fields.

I've also been thinking about the fact that in workshops I see work that knocks me flat, but whose creators are never heard from again. I don't think quiltmaking will ever have as large a group of recognized artists as painting does, because many

incredibly talented women do not have the drive, the organizing force, the tunnel vision, that it takes to be totally committed to an art. Nothing can compensate for the lack of that drive. Many women—and quilting remains primarily a women's art—can't see the importance of their work or perhaps can't afford to recognize it and what it would take to develop it fully.

It is interesting, in thinking back, that *Quilt National '81* had so many paintings that had been transformed into quilts. That was not the case in the 1983 exhibition. There was also less interest in innovative material for its own sake and less use of photo techniques and paper in the 1983 entries.

Like Pam Studstill and Michael James, I'm more of a colorist involved in the constant refining of color combinations and in classical ideas of color and shape that an artist can spend a lifetime working through. I love color and fabric, and ever since 1978 when I threw myself into quiltmaking full-time, I knew it was a lifetime commitment.

From my experience as a juror, workshop leader, and gallery-goer, I believe more good pieces are entered in *Quilt National* than in other exhibitions, a reflection of the prestige associated with what remains the only juried national show restricted to contemporary work.

I don't see a tremendous difference in the overall quality of the three *Quilt Nationals*. All had works displaying a balance of techniques and all had some outstanding pieces, some shocking ones, and some lemons. In every show—it doesn't matter what the medium—there are only a few works that stand out as strong individual pieces, and every juried show reflects a series of compromises.

The 1983 quilt artists, however, display a level of sophistication that was not there in 1979. The best people are getting more and more sophisticated —in techniques, color, composition, everything.

Joy Nixon

Patsy Allen
Greensboro, North Carolina
Deco Series #2
Cotton and cotton blends; machine-pieced, appliqued and quilted; 59" x 54". Photograph courtesy Brian Blauser.

As a contemporary art form, quilting has become far more accepted by the public, the art dealers, the galleries, and the collectors. When I began to exhibit work in the late 1970's, it was easier to make a splash because everything was still relatively new and not that many artists had turned to this form. Today, the work must be far more original. Then, it was easier to have impact because everything was so pastel and passive in the traditional quilt world.

The quilt artist has "arrived," and with acceptance has come more and more pressure to do better and better work—a challenge I think the contemporary quilt artist will welcome and accept.

A leader in the contemporary quilt world, Nancy Crow was a moving force behind the first *Quilt National* in 1979. She served as a juror for the 1981 exhibition and as a workshop leader for *Quilt National '83*. Her work has been shown in numerous invitational group and one-woman shows and is included in many public and private collections.

Joy Nixon

Contemporary quilting has, in a very few years, taken the quilt from its traditional use as bedcover or bed decoration. In quick succession, it has been applied first to walls, then to people; now the trend seems strongly oriented towards home decoration, with our entire environment fair game to the quilt artist. The quilting technique readily lends itself to modern adaptations, and I believe we will see a lot more contemporary quilting exploring the multiple-use idea.

There is a subtle sensuality in the tactile dimension provided by quilting which has an appeal to people on various levels. In these unsettling times, it can, for some, evoke warmth, comfort, security, tradition, and on-going continuity. For others, the quilt provides a marvelous vehicle to express their creativity.

In Canada, we have a growing number of seriously committed fibre artists, each working towards making a personal statement using piecework and quilting in various forms as a medium. Mixed media work is not as common as in the United States, but quilting is often used in conjunction with other fibre arts such as fabric painting and various needle arts to achieve the design.

The computer, too, is being enlisted in the quest for new design options, and I predict that it will be turned to increasingly to provide design stimulus.

We in Canada are definitely influenced by what we see happening in the United States. Canadians, however, work in greater isolation than their American cousins, and national exposure is more limited. This can have a positive side effect, as unique design ideas are being pursued which give a different flavour to quiltmaking in our country. Our unique natural environment often provides the inspiration for the quilt artist.

For Canadian quilt artists, the greatest challenge remains achieving recognition of quilting as an art form. Fortunately, exhibitions of the calibre of *Quilt National '83* will speed us toward our goal.

Joy Nixon, a native of Alberta, Canada, teaches extensively for the Adult Education Program in Calgary, offering courses in both traditional and contemporary quilting techniques. In recent years her own work has focused on quilted clothing, and her "quilts" are rarely seen in stationary exhibits. She was a workshop leader for *Quilt National '83*.

Marjorie Claybrook
Toledo, Ohio
The Amish Toucan
Hand-appliqued and quilted cotton African cloth, gauze,
jacquard, twills, calicos, and suede cloth; 76'' x 60''

The quilt was inspired by an Amish block-Roman stripe and my favorite bird, the toucan. Much of the fabric
was from earlier quilt projects, and even the feather ornament of the border had been used in other quilts.
From the beginning, "The Amish Toucan" brought smiles and laughter to beholders.

Nedra Carlson
Setauket, New York
Follow the Yellow Brick Road
Machine-pieced and machine-quilted cotton, cotton polyester
and rayon; cotton batting; 47" x 101"

While I approach the use of colors totally intuitively, the line design is thought out and drawn out very carefully
before I approach the fabrics I plan to use. I like to play with illusions to create a sense of motion and three-
dimensionality through both the interaction of colors and the line design itself.

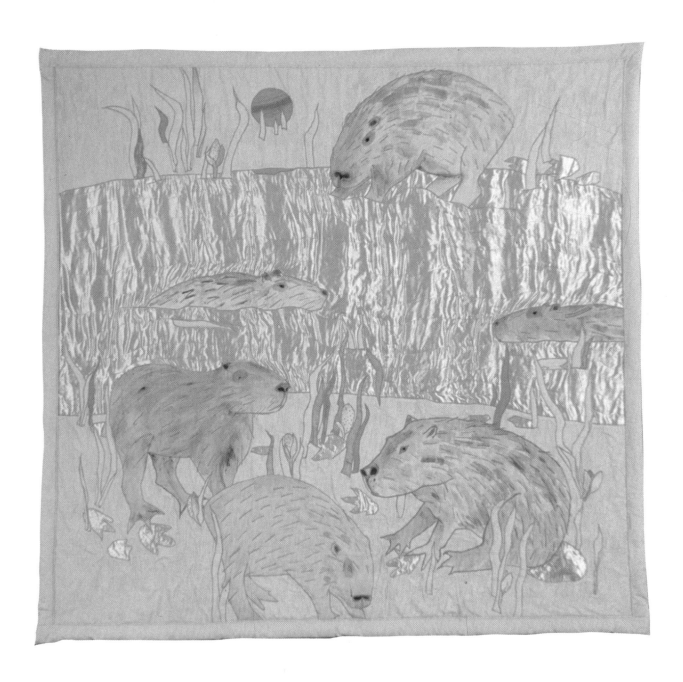

Nancy N. Erickson
Missoula, Montana
Jupiter Watch over Capybaraland
Painted and machine-stitched appliqued satins and cottons; 98" x 92"

Capybara, from South America, are the world's largest rodents. I first saw a pair at the Denver zoo. They are four feet or so in length, weigh up to 160 pounds, and are placid, intelligent, friendly, and communal. They make peculiar noises, live part time in the water, and (I've heard) can be trained as seeing-eye animals. They seemed so admirable and interesting that this piece resulted—and now a whole series of capybara pieces seems to be emerging.

Mary Bero
Madison, Wisconsin
Dream Dazzler
Machine-stitched procion-dyed strips of unbleached
muslin; 96" x 96"

This is my third quilt using dyed fabric strips from my "rag basket." The piece grew out of the eight-inch center square which was a reject from my second quilt. I had no set idea in mind when the quilt began; the piece just kept growing out from that center square, getting bolder and more visually shocking in its completing stages. I love how the center square pulls you in or on top of the quilt!

Jean Hewes
Los Gatos, California
Pillars
Machine-appliqued cotton, rayon, silk, polyester, brocades; 92" x 95"

I first assemble fabrics into a basic background cloth. I then pin the cloth to the batting and pin it to the wall. I then pin additional fabrics to the background and pin in a design to be machine-stitched.
Domini McCarthy Award for Exceptional Craftsmanship

Jean Hewes
Sticks
Machine-appliqued silk, rayon, brocades; 79" x 67"

Joyce Marquess Carey
Madison, Wisconsin
Tesselated Twill
Unbleached muslin base, appliqued with cotton strips
adhered to a grid of machine-sewn "graph paper"
lines; 84" x 72"

This piece is one of a series of self-portraits rendered in a variety of techniques. The image is derived from a computer-generated picture rendered in 22 shades of gray. "Tesselated Twill" is a combination of technology and fabric—the ultimate "software."

Donna J. Katz
Yellow Springs, Ohio
Dragonfly Paper
Hand-painted and hand-pieced fabric, hand-quilted; 72" x 72"

I like to combine diverse elements in order to discover new relationships and meanings. I use inanimate objects (*e.g.,* lawn chairs) in such a way that they take on expressionistic qualities usually associated with the human figure. Visually, I am interested in working with color, shape, and pattern.

Francoise Barnes
Athens, Ohio
Untitled
Machine-pieced and appliqued cotton and cotton blends; dacron
batting; 80" x 80"

Perhaps for the first time in my quiltmaking career, aesthetic appeal was not a concern as I worked on this piece; there were certain things that needed to be expressed and hopefully they were: Beauty and Elegance were not among them. The photographs by Malcolm Kirk in the book *Man as Art* (Viking Press) were an overwhelmingly inspiring starting point.
Invitational

Margaret Stephenson Coole
Mississauga, Ontario, Canada
Double Green Glazing
Cathedral window quilting, hand-dyed cotton with batik
inserts; 31" x 31"

I am fascinated by the rich sculptural surface of this fabric-manipulation unit, and the resulting grid allows exploration of spatial illusions through gradations of hue and value and/or pattern.

Ardyth Davis
Annandale, Virginia
Aurora II
Pure silk twill sprayed and brushed with dyes, pleated and
tied with cotton; cotton knit filling; 56" x 62"

My recent work in textiles has made use of elements of cloth to create textural fields. "Aurora II" evolved from
my earlier work using individual textile elements assembled into a large dimensional piece. It is one of a series
of quilts using large, whole pieces of painted cloth tied into pleats to make the repeating units. Tying in a
repeating pattern controls the cloth to some extent, yet it allows variation in the way the sections of fabric
fall—like so many structures occurring in nature which have certain controlling elements but have wide
variation in their form.

Nan Trichler
Willits, California
Black Cherry Swirl
Pieced, hand-quilted cotton; polyester batting; 74" x 58"

The quilt tradition is an honored heritage which also gives artists a basis from which to break free and pursue individual statements. With "Black Cherry Swirl," though, I found myself dipping deeper back into tradition; it was a sorting out of personal alliances with past images. After making a series of contemporary quilts, I felt a longing to return to older designs and ways. Still, I can see the modern influences I brought to working them.

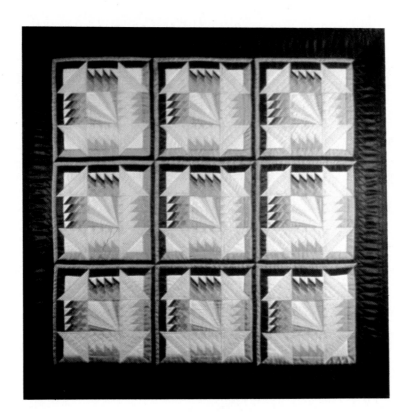

Virginia P. Lefferdink
New York, New York
Rain and Shine
Machine and hand-pieced cotton, silk, rayon, polyester; hand-quilted; 47" x 47"

The design's shapes, colors, and textures were chosen to suggest wetness, cloudiness, lightning, then sunbeams.

Dinah Prentice
Northampton, England
Perspective Drawing
Machine-pieced tussah and papillon silk drawn on with a spirit-based
ink and then washed to remove excess ink; 86" x 100"

I make quilts for philosophical reasons rather than functional ones.

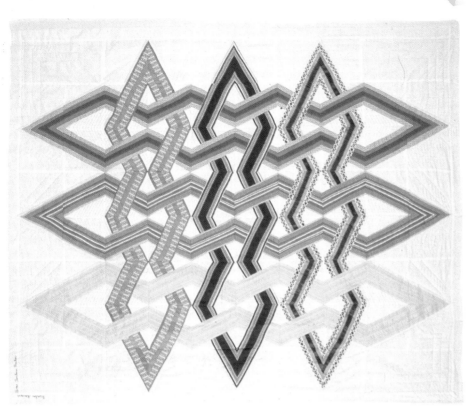

Barbara Packer
New York, New York
Rainbow Interweave
Machine strip-pieced, hand-quilted cottons and blends. Background is very old, fine bleached muslin; 80" x 66"

This quilt is one of several employing the same design explored through the use of different fabrics. The use of a strong solid color gives great impact to the basic line combined with various prints.

Barbara Packer
New York, New York
Interrupted Forward Progress
Machine-pieced and hand-quilted cottons and blends; 102" x 70"

This quilt is part of the artist's "Dusseldorf Series." All of the quilts in this series employ one basic block with variations which yield very different design results. The finished product appears very simple, but it is composed of about 4,000 separate pieces. The imposed grid gives the feeling of seeing two planes.

Connie Oliver
Pittsburgh, Pennsylvania
Folk Triptych: Johnny Appleseed, Joe Magarac & Mike Fink
Hand-appliqued and hand-quilted cotton and cotton blends (with
a small amount of machine-piecing); polyester batting; 66" x 84"

This piece is the first of two triptychs dealing with "larger than life" people who were either born in or
influenced the Western Pennsylvania area. Johnny Appleseed and Mike Fink were real men, one a gentle,
God-fearing man who loved and was loved by all God's creatures, the other a vicious scoundrel who typified the
scrappy keelboat men who opened up river commerce from Pittsburgh. These two flank the mighty Joe
Magarac, a mythic man made of the highest grade steel who could pour red-hot ingots with his bare hands. The
panels try to capture the spirit of each man, as well as a legendary moment in each of their lives.

Mary Lou Smith
Wilbraham, Massachusetts
Light in the Forest
Pieced cotton and blends; 39½" x 39½"

My biggest challenge in quiltmaking is to
tell a story or evoke a mood through the
use of traditional geometric quilt images
and traditional methods. My interest is not
so much in innovation as in reinterpreta-
tion and expansion of what has gone
before. This piece is the first of a series
depicting the changing seasons in northern
New England—in this case late summer/
early autumn.

Maryellen Hains
Kalamazoo, Michigan
Minimal One
Machine-pieced, hand-quilted cotton and
cotton blends; 78" x 72". Quilted by the
Miller family, Michigan Amish.

For the past three years I have been
exploring the use of crazy piecing to create
fabric that has a "painterly" quality. I
piece together dozens of fabrics that have
similar values. The shapes and scale of the
piecing are determined by the overall
image and effect of the projected quilt top.
"Minimal One's" dark background fabric
is crazy-pieced in large scale, and the
smaller "shots of light" are tiny pieces in
light and medium tones.

Ann Burian
Kalamazoo, Michigan
Ruth Zachary
Delton, Michigan
The Magic Carpet
Hand and machine applique and stitchery on rayon, silk,
cotton, metallics; beads, acrylic paint; 104'' x 104''

"The Magic Carpet" is intended to convey fairy tales as archetypal in the Jungian sense. Twelve blocks border
one side, representing 24 individual fairy tales. The other side features a central panel with a white knight motif
surrounded by nursery rhymes and more fairy tale motifs. The overall effect is that of a Persian carpet. The
piece was originally conceived of as a special feature in an exhibition of ritual and ceremonial capes based on
archetypal images. "The Magic Carpet" was worked fully and equally by both artists.

Sara Long
Fort Bragg, California
Indian Blanket
Pieced and hand-quilted cotton and cotton blends; polyester
batting; 70'' x 48'' (hanging size: 48'' x 35'')

This quilt was made as an offering of thanks to the American Indian spirit.

Janice Anthony
Brooks, Maine
Great Wall of China
Machine and hand-pieced, hand-quilted cotton; polyester batting; 85" x 82"

The Great Wall fascinated me because it seems to have its own invisible life—ageless, transcending its human makers to be the only man-made object visible from space. Its weighty stone fortresses contrast with its delicacy of line, flowing serenely across the landscape for 1,400 miles.

Jody Klein
Waltham, Massachusetts
108 Cows with Silver Tails
Paper bonded to fabric; stamped, stitched on silk and paper; painted, drawn, stuffed; machine-stitched; wrapped tails; 48" x 47"

The imaging of fabric or paper with rubber stamps is a process in which the "one inking, one impression" yields images which are both the same and unique. The use of paper in quilts was inspired by the use of paper templates in traditional quilt techniques, especially when the paper was left in the quilt. Turning this idea "inside out" resulted in a series of paper quilts, of which "108 Cows with Silver Tails" is one. The quilt's design is inspired by the traditional "Robbing Peter to Pay Paul" design.

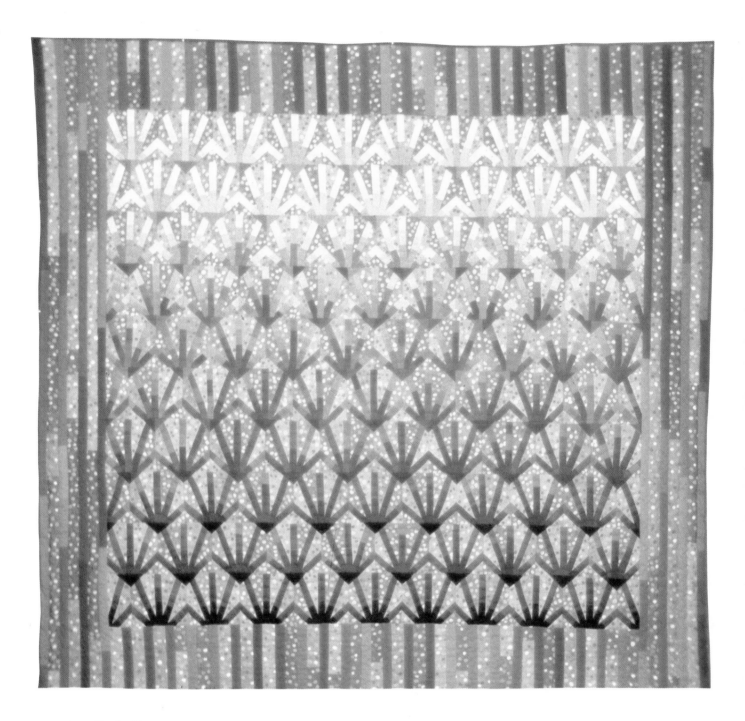

Pam Studstill
San Antonio, Texas
Quilt # 21
Hand-painted, hand-quilted, machine-pieced cottons; synthetic
batting; 53" x 53"

I like to play with color gradations, sometimes working within the limitations of commercially-dyed fabrics, sometimes dyeing the fabric myself. The surface paint not only creates a random pattern but also helps ease the transition from color to color. I am inspired by landscape views and vistas, fields of anything, all the quilts I've ever seen, and looking at my boxes of colored material.

Best of Show Award

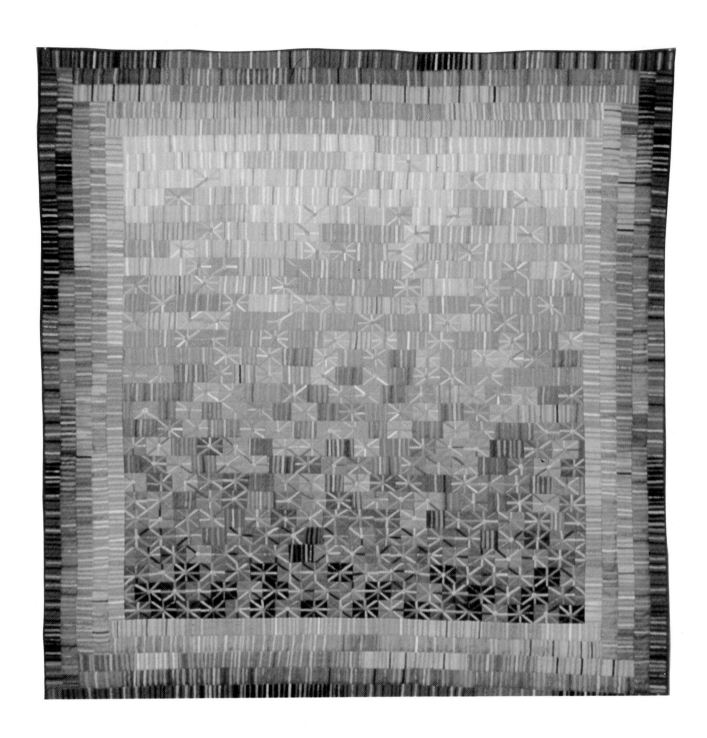

Pam Studstill
Quilt # 22
Quilted by Bettie Studstill.
51" x 54"

Best of Show Award

B.J. Elvgren
Pittsburgh, Pennsylvania
The Twelve Days of Christmas
Hand-pieced, hand-quilted cotton, cotton blends, velvet, silk,
and satin; some machine-piecing on the border; border brackets
are trapunto; 100" x 108"

"The Twelve Days of Christmas" is based on the traditional song. The quilt is conceived as a joyful celebration
of gift-giving, with the greatest gift of all being the Holy Child.

People's Choice Award

Karen Grier
Miami, Florida
Painted Bunting
Strip-pieced, hand-quilted cotton and cotton blends; cotton/polyester batting; 56" x 46"

The coloration for this piece was inspired by the painted bunting, one of North America's most beautiful birds. The piece was designed with two separate functions in mind. It may be opened flat and displayed as a two-dimensional wall hanging or folded in half, tied, and worn as a reversible "body-quilt" or kimono designed to adorn the human figure in the bunting's plumage.

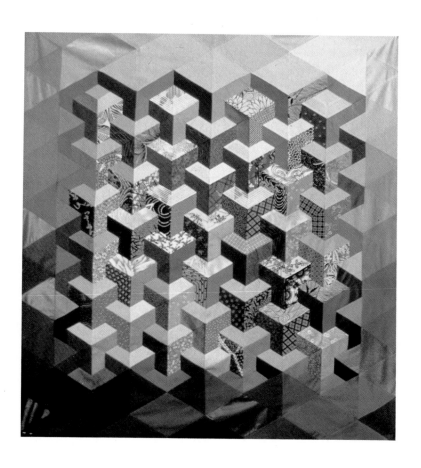

Miriam Nathan-Roberts
Berkeley, California
Kyoto
Machine-pieced Japanese cotton kimono fabrics and cotton and blends; hand-quilted by Lizzie Kurtz; 50" x 50"

My aim is to produce a sense of three-dimensionality using one geometric shape and combining traditional cotton prints and solids with Japanese cotton kimono fabric. The light source is to be perceived as coming from the upper right. As I approached the border I wanted the "buildings" to expand in size until they appeared to dissolve into fractured light.

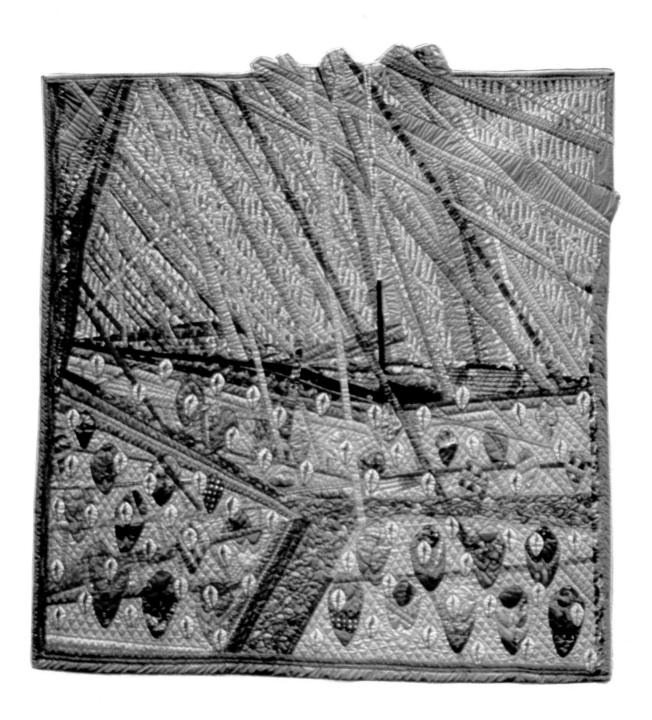

Terrie Hancock Mangat
Cincinnati, Ohio
Sunny Day on Cochina Beach
Cotton blends and embroidery thread; the quilt was pieced,
cut apart, and repieced; appliqued shells; quilted by Sue Rule;
57½" x 57"

This quilt was inspired by an adventure in gathering live cochina shells for a cochina chowder. The sky has rays of yellow sun cutting through the warm blue sky to the beach where the shells are in thousands. The T-shaped vein of tiny embroidered shells represents that rich, thick vein of shells one finds when digging down into the sand near the water's edge.

Terrie Hancock Mangat
Fishing Hats over Rose Lake
Cotton blends, rose appliques, sequins; the hats have various
plastic and rubber artifacts sewn on them; main technique is
reverse applique; quilted by Sue Rule; 82" x 75"

All of the shapes floating in the sky over Rose Lake are the parts of a fishing hat which I was duplicating for a
friend. The shapes are done in five different sizes, to give the feeling of depth. The roses are feminine in feeling
and the grasses are masculine. Above the quilt are the real fishing hats.

Most Innovative Use of the Medium Award

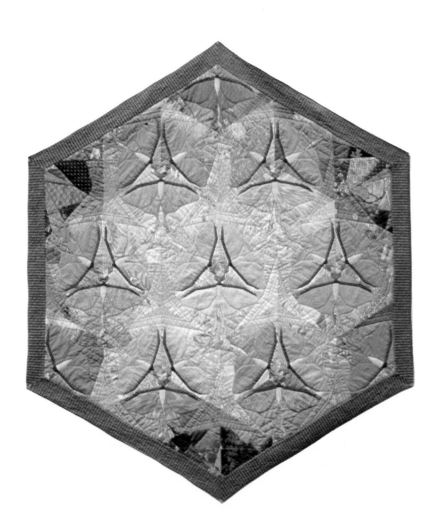

Ruth B. McDowell
Winchester, Massachusetts
Luna Moths
Machine-pieced, hand-quilted cottons, synthetics, blends, flannel; 61" x 52"

This quilt grew out of a study of the 17 symmetries of a plane and a fascination with this beautiful pale green insect with furry body and fern-like antennae. The moth exhibits mirror symmetry and is used in this quilt in the arrangement known as p3m1.

Judi Warren
Maumee, Ohio
Interior/Exterior Windowscape; Grass and Glass
Pieced and appliqued cottons and viscose satin; some hand-dyed; 46" x 47"

The "window" theme has been a recurring image in my paintings and drawings. Translating that image into quilted fabric gives it new excitement. Working with hand-dyed colors is somewhat like painting, and the quilting creates subtleties much the same as embellishments in a drawing. In the quilt I find an added quality of contrast between the soft light-and-shadow of the quilting and the clean edges of the pictorial statement.

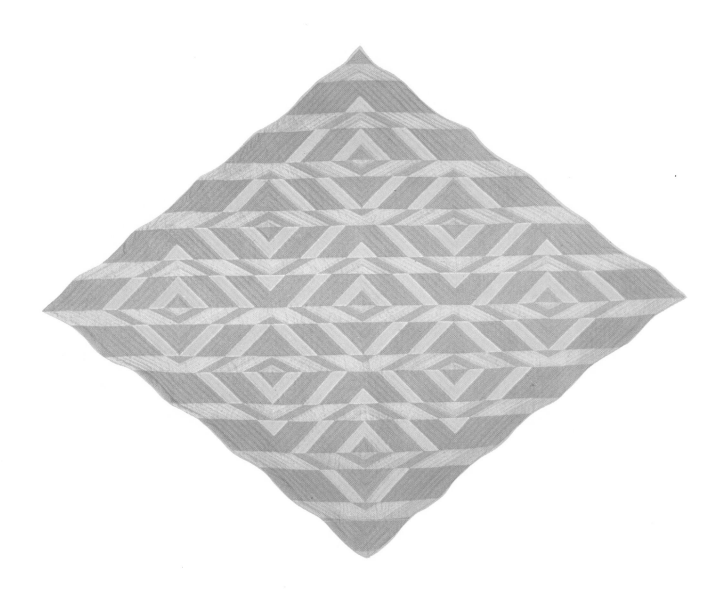

Peggy Spaeth
Cleveland Heights, Ohio
Dodecagons'
Hand-pieced, hand-quilted cotton; polyester batting; 81" x 63"

Joyce Parr
Gambier, Ohio
Jacob's Ladder
Machine-pieced, hand-appliqued, hand-quilted cotton;
cotton batting; 52" x 52"

This quilt began as a machine-pieced crazy quilt. I kept adding pieces, appliqueing them by hand, until I felt satisfied. Then I hand-quilted it, designing the pattern as I went along. The "Jacob's Ladder" idea is one I have worked out in other variations. The ladder is a symbol of aspirations, a connecting, and a making possible of things which may have seemed out of reach. There is something comforting about putting it all into a quilt.

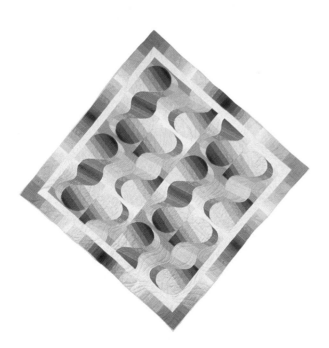

Gerlinde Anderson
Old Town, Maine
Flamingos Along the Shore
Cottons, chintz, curved seams with strip-piecing; polyester batting; 60" x 60"

Unlike my other work, this quilt was originally conceived as an exercise in curved seams and strip-piecing with polychromatic gradations. While it was developing, however, images of graceful flamingos flying over shallow waters came to mind. As flamingos are not native to Maine, I must have been inspired by the plastic flamingos that live on the lawns along our coastline.

Kathleen Moore Farling
Oxford, Ohio
Indigo and Shibori Quilt with Kanoko Dots
Hand-quilted cotton, hand-pieced border; indigo immersion dyebath; tie-dye and stitch-resist techniques; polyester batting; 66" x 43½"

Shibori is a Japanese term for tie-dye and stitch-resist dyeing. While exploring the various methods by which selected areas of fabric could be kept free of dye, I was intrigued with the possibilities of using figurative line and creating spatial illusion, of contrasting dense pattern and open planes. Technically, the ribbon-like lines were created with tightly gathered running stitches; the dots by wrapping many small pucker points (*Kanoko* technique); and the border by diagonally wrapping fabric around a pole, lashing it, and condensing the fabric into pleats (*Arashi* technique) prior to immersion in the indigo dye bath.

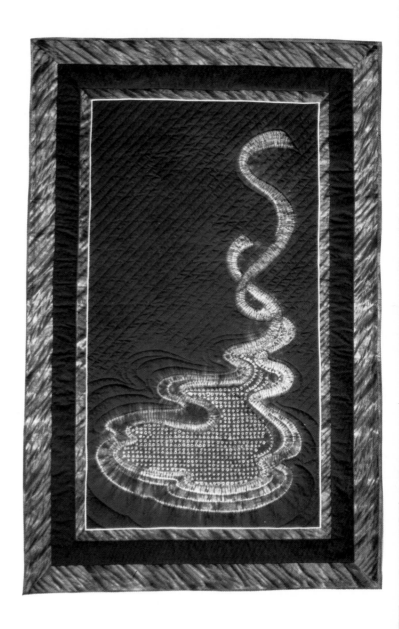

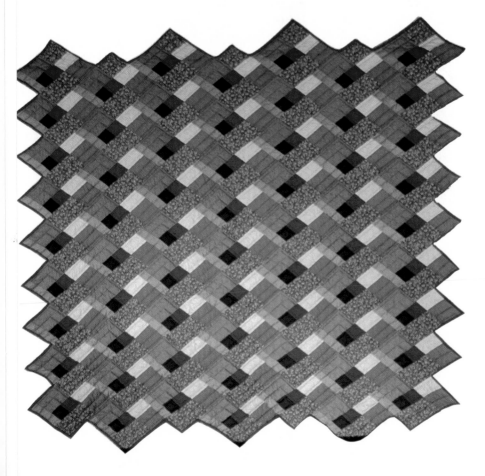

Andrea Leong Scadden
Seattle, Washington
Night Flight
Machine-pieced, hand-quilted cotton and
cotton polyester; 62" x 69"

In "Night Flight" I hoped to capture the
feeling of dynamic motion as inspired by
the thousands of Canadian geese that in
late autumn launch themselves at day-
break from Nebraska ponds in their
southern migration.

Pat Cody
Fort Worth, Texas
Deco Diamonds
Machine-pieced, hand-quilted cotton;
bonded polyester batting; 72" x 76"

In this piece, Art Deco influence shows
strongly in the diamond angles, the zig-zag
piecing patterns, and the counterpoint
lines of the quilting design. The contemporary abruptness of the Art Deco theme
is softened—echoing the heritage of quilts
before it—by fabric and color choices.

Tana Krizova-Lizon
Knoxville, Tennessee
Space I
White cotton background; heat-transferred fabric
crayon drawings; stretched on frame; 24" x 24"

Using fabric crayons, I wanted to get almost painterly images, which are hard to get with just plain color fabric. This is my first work in this direction; before this my work had more hard edges. Some areas I stuffed to get another pigmentation and more softness. As light changes the quilt changes too. I like the idea of figures coming out of the surface and fading back just like everything is around us in space.

Gail A. Hanson
Bloomington, Minnesota
Be the First to Get Your Marbles Home
Machine-pieced and quilted cotton and cotton blends; 75" x 41½"

This quilt is an experiment in "weaving" on a sewing machine. The colors are arranged as if woven on a loom. As for the name, the finished product reminded me of the pathways on a child's gameboard. The brighter areas seemed to shine as in a glass surface; thus "Be the First to Get Your Marbles Home."

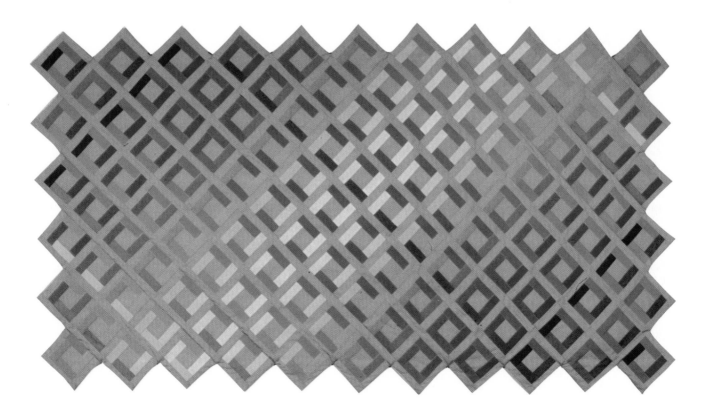

Kay Parker
Ithaca, New York
Whales and Snails
Machine-pieced, hand-quilted cotton/ polyester; polyester batting; 73" x 73"

"Whales and Snails" is representative of my work, which focuses on a type of pattern known as a "tessellation." A tessellation is made of interlocking and repeating shapes that cover a flat surface without overlapping or leaving gaps. The word stems from the Latin *tessellae,* meaning tiling. The creation of a continuous piece of fabric from smaller pieces is analagous to the building of a tile mosaic, and piecing together a patchwork quilt is essentially creating a cloth mosaic.

Karen Lynn Murray
Syracuse, New York
Transition # 7
Machine strip-pieced, hand-quilted cotton and blends, some over-dyed; cotton/polyester batting; 53½" x 58½"

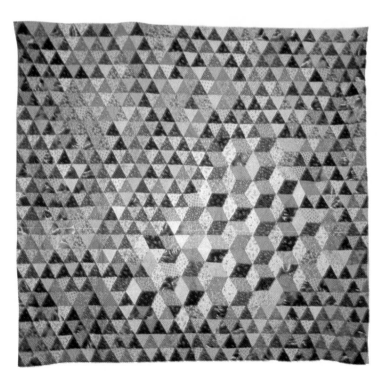

Basically my work is about illusion. I use color and value to create areas that appear three-dimensional and contrast them with areas that are more two-dimensional. My aim is to apply the principles of illusion traditionally used in painting to patchwork and patterning.

Virginia Jacobs
Philadelphia, Pennsylvania
1FQ83 - Magic Carpet
Machine-pieced and quilted nylon flag bunting and lame (battery-
operated lights for night flying); 108" x 60"

The idea for this piece arose last year while I was abroad. My visit was fascinating in all, but at one point I really just wanted to go home. Then I realized what that would involve and that what I wanted, more correctly, was simply to *be* home. My incandescent flying quilt is my imaginary improvement over the actualities of contemporary travel.

Invitational

47

Michael James
Somerset Village, Massachusetts
La Tempete (The Storm)
Machine-pieced, machine-quilted cotton; cotton/polyester
batting; 78" x 86"

In the last year I have deliberately moved away from the preciousness of hand-sewing processes in order to force the viewer to confront the two-dimensional surface image. I am impatient with individuals whose obsession with tiny stitches and intricate quilting patterns interferes with their contemplation of the design. For me, my quilts are flexible supports for patterns painted with strips of fabric color.

Invitational

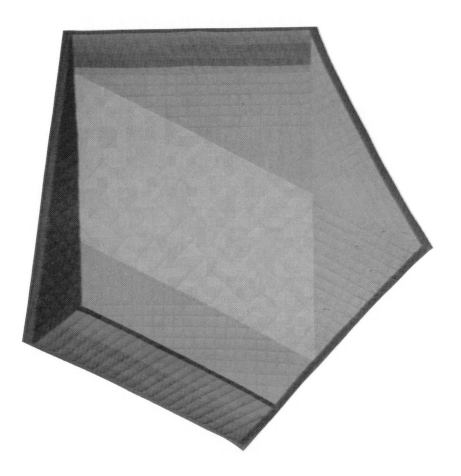

Debra Millard
Englewood, Colorado
Penta-Squares
Machine-pieced, hand-quilted cotton muslin, hand-dyed with procion fiber-reactive dyes; 42" x 40"

The subtle colors are achieved by hand-dyeing the fabric with evenly spaced gradations from light to dark values in seven different hues. The juxtaposition of the pieced areas with the solid areas helps to achieve the three-dimensional quality. The irregular outside shape evolved from my enjoyment of the styles of the Art Deco period and the Constructivist painters of the 1920s.

Sharon R. Myers
Concord, New Hampshire
Wauwinet Sky
Machine-pieced, hand-dyed, hand-quilted cotton chintz; 54" x 54"

Here I have tried to recreate my own experience of being transported by the softness of light and color at sunset to a place so tranquil it can only be reached in the stillness of evening.

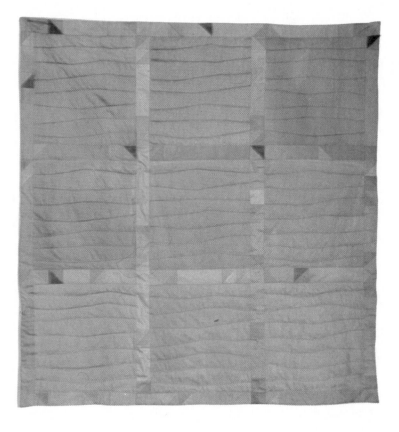

Judy B. Dales
Boonton Township, New Jersey
Pale Reflections
Hand-pieced, hand-quilted cotton and cotton-poly blends; polyester batting; 56" x 56"

"Pale Reflections," inspired by Islamic geometric designs, is based on a circle. The subdued color scheme was chosen to enhance and emphasize the one print used, which is one of my favorites. The quilting was done free-form, following the pieced design.

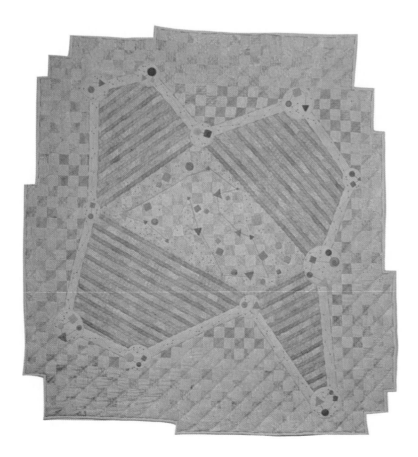

Sandra Humberson
Friendsville, Maryland
Star Map
Hand screen-printed fabrics; pieced, hand and machine embroidery; hand and machine-quilted; 76" x 72"

"Star Map" originated from a drawing I did in 1975. I pulled it out from time to time and it seemed new and fresh each time. In 1978 I started working with imaginary map images and made several large quilted pieces with irregular edges. In 1979 I decided the drawing should be a quilt using hand-embroidery as the dominant technique. I finished the stitching of the four-sided central part and put it away until January 1982, when it became quite important to me to complete the piece.

Linda MacDonald
Willits, California
Ruth Fresno's Dream
Pieced and appliqued cotton; bonded
polyester batting; 82" x 82"

"Ruth Fresno's Dream" is a study in
juxtaposed space, pattern, dimension,
subtle colors and the relationship among
all of these. The quilting, in two combined
colors, adds the dimension, the definition,
the frill, while always remaining the
essence of what makes a quilt a quilt.

Rhonda Cunha
Amherst, Massachusetts
Blue Loops
Unfinished muslin, hand-dyed; base and
three-dimensional units machine-sewed;
galvanized steel wire inserted into the loop
seam allowances; 80" x 54½"

My work often focuses on repeated units or
shapes, and color arrangements which
form entirely new shapes within the
composition. As the viewer walks from one
side of "Blue Loops" to another, subtle
changes occur in the light, color, and
pattern. From the front, the piece appears
two-dimensional and works as a quilt;
from either side, it becomes a piece of
sculpture.

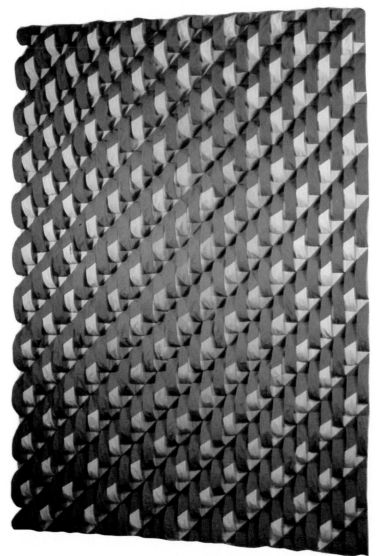

Therese May
San Jose, California
Monster Quilt # 1
Muslin border, gessoed and painted with acrylic; center portion
appliqued with satin stitch and painted with acrylic; 46" x 51"

This quilt shows a braided rug pattern surrounding some rather ambiguous figurations. In appliqueing the fabric pieces I let the threads hang loose to form a kind of network that starts to reveal the sewing process. I have covered the border completely with acrylic paint (and monster imagery), and the center pieced portion with small dabs of paint, not only to enhance the surface but also to bring my quilting techniques and painting techniques closer together. The intent is to help confuse the issues often raised about "art vs. craft."

Patsy Allen
Greensboro, North Carolina
Deco Series # 2
Machine-pieced, appliqued and quilted cotton, blends; polyester batting; 59" x 54"

"Deco Series #2" is part of a new group of quilts I began as a result of my interest in geometric design and the Art Deco period of the 1920s and 1930s. The quilts utilize the colors and motifs of that period of art and also incorporate the themes of pattern and spatial relationships with which I generally work. I thoroughly enjoy what I do and I hope that comes across to the viewer.

Jeannie M. Spears
St. Paul, Minnesota
Delectable Mountains Dreamed
Hand-quilted unbleached muslin, folded, stitched, and dyed; block print using direct dyes; 100" x 86"

"Delectable Mountains Dreamed" is an interpretation in hand-dyed fabrics of a traditional pattern. The original quilt was a prizewinner in the 1939 Sears Chicago World's Fair Contest. I folded the fabric and stitched the quilting line through all the layers before dyeing the background (sky) areas. The mountains were printed using a felt and acrylic block.

Buff Hungerland
Mercer Island, Washington
Auras & Edges
Airbrush/stencil; machine-pieced, hand-quilted cotton; polyester
batting; 50" x 40"

I've been fascinated by the edges of things since noticing the edges of handmade paper: all the complexities and ingredients are revealed. Fiber art is the medium of my choice, and I began to question the traditional treatment of fabric edges—turned in and under, hidden—and in my non-functional pieces I began to use the juxtaposition of stenciled/airbrushed hard edges with the soft revealed edges of torn cotton. The kinetic possibilities of the torn strips appeal to me, as do the possibilities of relating my exploration of edges to the human condition.

Marilyn McKenzie Chaffee
San Diego, California
Del Rio Quilt
Hand-quilted cotton and cotton blends; 50" x 50"

Sources of inspiration are sometimes lofty, sometimes mundane. This quilt was designed around a marvelous remnant of fabric that caught my eye in a local dime store basement.

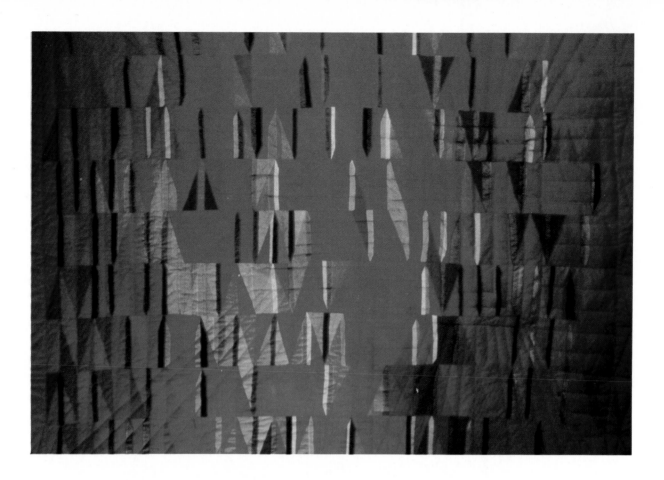

Judith Larzelere
Newburyport, Massachusetts
Summer
Machine-pieced, hand-quilted cotton;
polyester batting; 96" x 78"

"Summer" is one of a four-part series on
the seasons, and in it I wanted to interpret
my color sense of July/August when the
sun shines so brightly and the heat is most
intense. I used complementary colors and
a flickering placement of strips to help add
dazzle to the piece. The quilting design
was inspired by a painting by F.S.
Hundertwasser.

Lucretia Romey
Canton, New York
Diagonal Barns
Hand-sewn cotton and cotton blends;
polyester batting; 60" x 48"

I hand-sew a quilt as I would paint a
picture. I choose 30 or 40 pieces of fabric
and from each cut long strips of cloth.
With a rough sketch as a guide, I sew these
directly on top of backing and fiberfill as a
painter would select a color and apply a
brush stroke to paper or canvas.

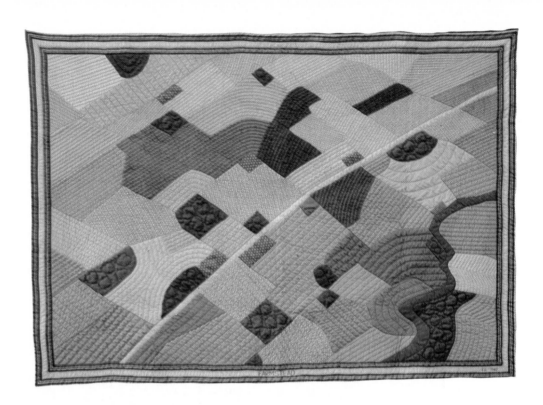

Flavin Glover
Auburn, Alabama
Farmstead
Hand-appliqued, hand-quilted cotton and cotton blends; polyester batting; 46" x 62"

"Farmstead" depicts an aerial view of farm country. Patches of fabric were appliqued together to form the composition, and quilting lines create the illusion of fields, furrows, and rows. Farm country is much like a natural patchwork pattern that continuously changes with the seasons.

Rebekka Seigel
Owenton, Kentucky
Duck Pond
Cotton, polyester, rayon, batik, direct dye, reverse applique, Seminole patchwork; 108" x 85"

While watching ducks swimming, dragonflies scooting, and frogs jumping on my pond one summer day, I was struck by the teeming of life in such a small area and decided I needed to make a quilt about it. This quilt is my attempt to represent the feeling of lush coolness and peace I get when surrounded by hues of blue and green.

Esther Parkhurst
Los Angeles, California
Joseph's Coat
Machine-pieced, hand-quilted, strip-pieced cotton, cut and sewn
several times; 55" x 70"

I used this technique because I wanted to achieve the effect that certain parts were floating in an opposite direction and to create movement simultaneously.

58

Nancy Crow
Baltimore, Ohio
Tramp Art I
Machine-pieced and strip-pieced cotton and cotton blends; polyester
batting; hand-quilted by Rose Augenstein; 63'' x 56''

I am intrigued by Tramp Art, which was made during the late 1800's and up through the early part of this
century. In a fit of enlightenment, I realized I too liked making bigger shapes out of bits and pieces. It is
absorbing to keep adding—and then adding more—behavior completely related to my strong tendency to
clutter.

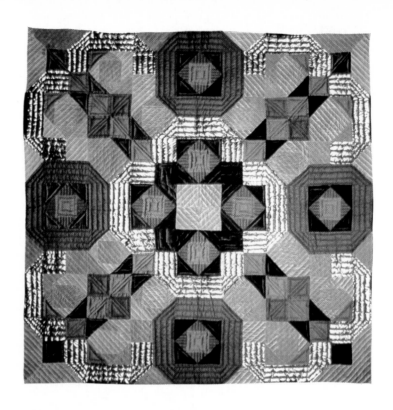

Ruth Smiler
Montpelier, Vermont
Matrix III
Machine-pieced, hand-quilted cotton velvet, broadcloth, metallic vinyl bonded to woven cotton; 64'' x 64''

"Matrix III" is one of a series in which I was beginning to explore the light-reflective characteristics of different fabric textures and contrasting these with metallic materials.

Christine Holst
Nantucket, Massachusetts
Watching T.V.
Appliqued and pieced cottons, polyblends, silks; hand-quilted; 64'' x 50''

This quilt was inspired by my living with a color television for the first time.

Joy Nixon
Calgary, Alberta, Canada
On the Line
Log cabin insets, Seminole piecing and channel quilting;
100 percent cotton.

My initial concept was to fashion a jacket using as many quilting techniques as possible, keeping in mind the boundaries set by the geometry and size of the finished piece.

Invitational

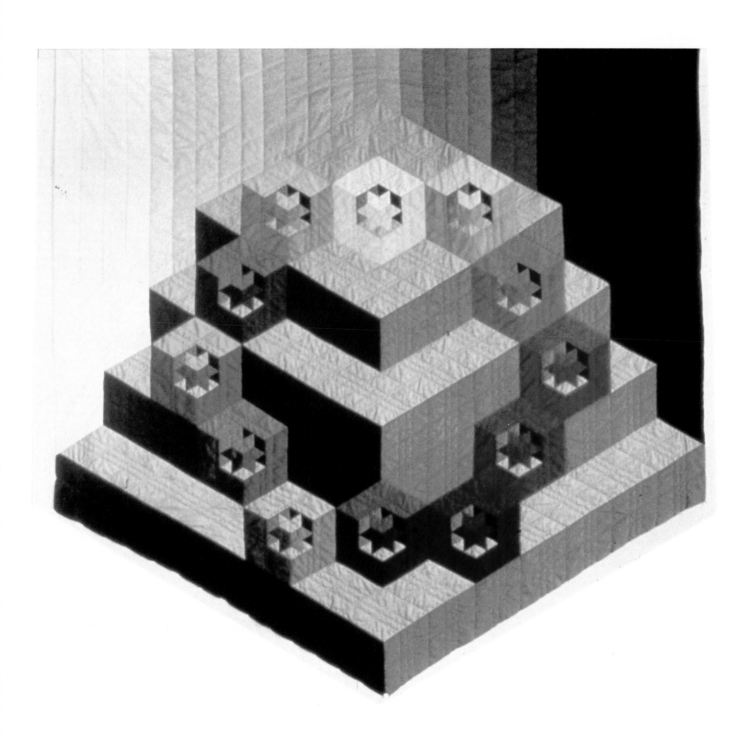

Chris Wolf Edmonds
Lawrence, Kansas
Night Rainbow II: A Place for Everything and Everything in Its Place
Hand and machine-pieced, hand-quilted cotton; 50" x 50"

The illusion of three-dimensional space and form is achieved through the use of three values of each color and the system of isometric projection.

Pauline Burbidge
Nottingham, England
Cubic Log Cabin
Machine-pieced and machine-quilted cottons, most of which are
hand-dyed; cotton batting; 71" x 66"

Both "Cubic Log Cabin" and "Cubic Pyramid" are designed on a theme of three-dimensional illusion, using flat pattern to indicate a 3-D effect. I took the idea of the traditional "Tumbling Blocks" design and took it a few stages further. Almost all the fabrics are hand-dyed, and the use of colour and tone are equally as important as the shapes.

Award of Excellence

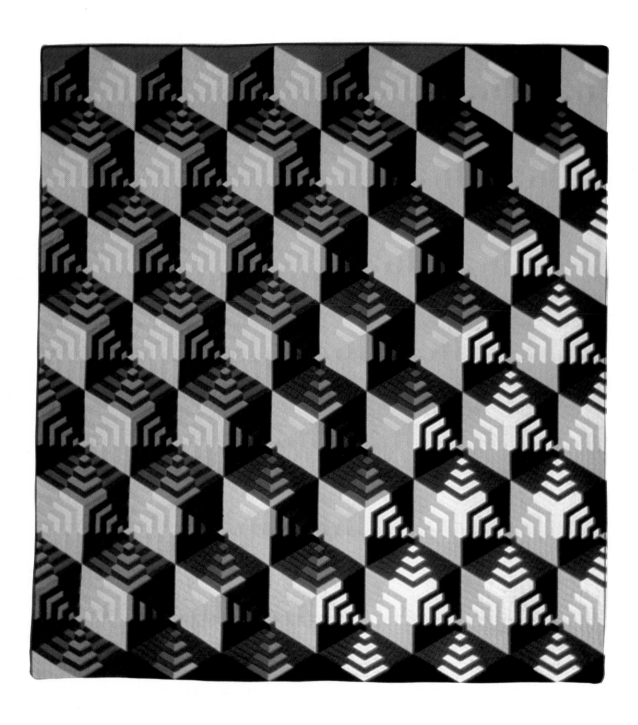

Pauline Burbidge
Cubic Pyramid
Machine-pieced and machine-quilted cotton fabrics, most of which
are hand-dyed; cotton batting; 86½" x 80"

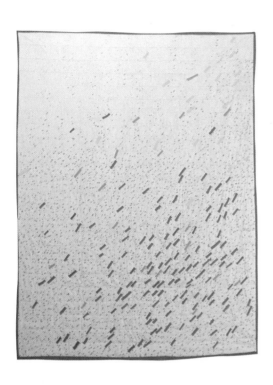

Patricia J. Pauly
Rochester, New York
Dashes
Hand-silkscreened main ground; "dashes" hand-appliqued in cotton and poly/cotton blends; hand-quilted; polyester fiber-fill batting; 52" x 40½"

In "Dashes" I was interested in repeating the hand-screened pattern found in the background. The hand-appliqued colors give that detail I wanted. This quilt shows the "painterly" quality of my work.

Catherine Joslyn
Clarion, Pennsylvania
Akan Tribute
Artist-dyed mercerized 100 percent cotton sateen; polyester batting; 85" x 60"

The Akan people of Ghana (the old "Gold Coast" of West Africa) include the Ashanti, Fanti, and Anyi. The quilt's design was inspired by the Akan strip-woven ritual cloth called *kente*.

Lisa N. Coleman
St. Louis, Missouri
Hickety-Pickety
Hand and machine-quilted cotton velveteen squares, hand-painted
with procion dyes; machine-appliqued lettering; chintz border;
polyester batting; 94" x 78"

Nostalgic feelings of warmth, of my 1950s childhood fun, emerge with the memory of a soft, thick blanket, tacked together with yarn and printed in an overall "Ball and Jacks" pattern. The printed fabric alone seems to evoke all that was good in childhood: security, innocence, uninhibited play. "Hickety-Pickety" reflects a personal need to recapture similar feelings in my work through the playful construction of a thick comforter. It is a peculiar nursery rhyme, written in a nearly illegible "chicken scrawl"; a humorous series of snapshot-like chicken imagery.

Marion L. Huyck
Evanston, Illinois
Russian Medallion
Hand-appliqued, machine-pieced, hand-quilted cotton; polyester
batting; 94" x 66"

While doing research on children's literature, I was particularly drawn to the work of Ivan Bilibin (1867 - 1942), a Russian graphic artist and stage designer whose style is rooted in Russian folk art and medieval art. For this quilt, the medallion format offered the greatest flexibility in experimenting with border designs. Although I do preliminary sketches and proportioning on graph paper, I select colors intuitively, working from the center out. Quilted filler designs are suggestive of traditional folk art patterns. I free-hand sketched the quilted castles and village to suggest the landscapes that inspired Bilibin.

Quilt National '83 Installation. Photograph courtesy of Brian Blauser.

THE DAIRY BARN

The Dairy Barn, Southeastern Ohio Cultural Arts Center, is dedicated to producing exhibitions of high quality and innovative programs featuring both traditional and contemporary fine and cultural arts.

The Barn dates back to 1914 and is a classic example of barn architecture of that era. It was built to house dairy cattle as part of the Athens Mental Health Center's activity therapy program and for years was noted for its outstanding herds.

In 1977 when the State of Ohio announced plans to raze the structure, local citizens rallied to save it. They succeeded and immediately began the Barn's transformation into a cultural arts center for the region. In 1978, the Dairy Barn was placed on the National Register of Historic Places.

The structure is 200 feet long by 35 feet wide, has 14,000 square feet of floor space, and is undergoing a continual process of renovation as funding becomes available. Plans range from the basic—the installation of a heating system and a system of movable walls—to the more ambitious. These include conversion of the huge second-floor hayloft to usable space and creation of an amphitheater for performing arts and space for marketing regional arts and crafts.

Organized as a non-profit corporation and dependent largely on volunteers, the Dairy Barn is supported by admission and membership fees, government and private grants, and corporate and individual contributions.

Part of the Dairy Barn's indisputable charm is its setting in the Appalachian foothills, with cattle still grazing close enough to view and be viewed by visitors to exhibitions.

The Dairy Barn is proud that through its three *Quilt National* exhibitions and their accompanying lectures, workshops, and publications, it has played a major role in showcasing and promoting contemporary quilting as a lively and challenging art form.

Exhibition Designer Statement
Doreen Strasser-Pallini

As exhibition designer for *Quilt National '79, '81,* and *'83,* I have been responsible for preparing installations which visually project the philosophical concepts underlying the exhibition.

From *Quilt National's* inception, the intent was to bring the contemporary quilt into the mainstream of the fine arts and to present it as a medium possible of great depth and diversification. The installation had to present the contemporary quilt as an aesthetic entity which could exist away from its traditional function as a bed ornament or covering.

The Dairy Barn space is a huge, white room with numerous windows and very limited wall space. The quilts could have hung soldier-like around the Barn, reminiscent of traditional quilts strung on a clothesline or of traditional quilt exhibitions. Each quilt would then have presented its face to the same lighting and to the same viewpoint. But I was too conscious of each quilt's individuality.

From working with the quilts I knew the variations of their textures, the characteristics of their surfaces, their weight and thickness, their colors. Even their fragrances were part of my experience. Each was an original design created from a need for personal expression and realized in a variety of materials. Each had to be installed in a way which would emphasize its uniqueness.

Therefore, I hung the quilts on rods and suspended them from the Barn's ceiling in a sculptural configuration that was, of course, different for each exhibition. The unity of the *Quilt*

National '83 installation was achieved through coordination of color and relationship of form. Of prime importance was that each quilt should exist in its own space. Even the back of almost every quilt could be viewed, making the observer more aware of the technique which created its structure. Each work could be viewed closely and totally.

From the first quilt I received in 1979 for the first *Quilt National,* I was aware that these works were the seeds of new beginnings for the quilt. It was this awareness that guided my attempts to convey the significance of each work.

The Dairy Barn Southeastern Ohio Cultural Arts Center, Athens, Ohio. Photograph courtesy of C.H. Merkle.

INDEX